Shambhala Dragon Editions

The dragon is an age-old symbol of the highest spiritual essence, embodying wisdom, strength, and the divine power of transformation. In this spirit, Shambhala Dragon Editions offers a treasury of readings in the sacred knowledge of Asia. In presenting the works of authors both ancient and modern, we seek to make these teachings accessible to lovers of wisdom everywhere.

THE HEART OF AWARENESS

A Translation of the *Ashtavakra Gita*

Thomas Byrom

Foreword by J. L. Brockington

SHAMBHALA
Boston & Shaftesbury
1990

Shambhala Publications, Inc.
Horticultural Hall
300 Massachusetts Avenue
Boston, Massachusetts 02115

Shambhala Publications, Inc.
The Old School House
The Courtyard, Bell Street
Shaftesbury, Dorset SP7 8BP

9 8 7 6 5 4 3 2 1

First Edition
Printed in the United States of America on acid-free paper
Distributed in the United States by Random House
and in Canada by Random House of Canada Ltd.
Distributed in the United Kingdom by Element Books Ltd.

Library of Congress Cataloging-in-Publication Data
Aṣṭāvakragītā. English.
The heart of awareness: a translation of the Ashtavakra Gita / Thomas Byrom; foreword by J. L. Brockington.
—1st ed.
p. cm.
ISBN 1-57062-643-X
1. Advaita. 2. Vedanta. 3. Absolute, The. 4. Self-realization. I. Byrom, Thomas. II. Title.
B132.A3A7413 1990 89-43512
181′.482—dc20 CIP

priyāyā māyāyā
caraṇakamalābhyāṃ tasya hṛdi
punaḥ punar namāmi

For my Beloved Ma.
At Her feet, in His heart
again and again I bow.

Contents

Foreword ix
Acknowledgments xv
Translator's Introduction: The Mystery of Awareness xvii
1. The Self 1
2. Awareness 6
3. Wisdom 12
4. The True Seeker 15
5. Dissolving 17
6. Knowledge 18
7. The Boundless Ocean 20
8. The Mind 22
9. Dispassion 24
10. Desire 26
11. Stillness 28
12. Fulfillment 31
13. Happiness 33
14. The Fool 35
15. The Clear Space of Awareness 36
16. Forget Everything 42
17. Beyond All 45
18. The Master 50
19. My Own Splendor 72
20. I Am Shiva 74
Notes 79

Foreword

The *Aṣṭāvakragītā,* which Dr. Byrom has so ably translated here, is known under several different names, for example, *Adhyātmaśāstra, Avadhūtānubhūti, Jñānānandasamuccaya* and so forth, as well as variants on the *Aṣṭāvakragītā* title such as *Aṣṭāvakrasūkta* and *Aṣṭāvakrasaṃhitā.* This variation in its naming suggests its essential anonymity—a feature which superficially would link it with the "anonymous literature" par excellence of the Epics and Purāṇas, as would also both parts of the name *Aṣṭāvakragītā.* There have been, of course, numerous texts called Gītās, composed in imitation of the *Bhagavadgītā,* which is perhaps the most famous single part of the *Mahābhārata,* and most of these are (or at any rate claim to be) incorporated in one or another of the Purāṇas. There are, however, a few Gītās which make no such claim but are fully independent, and it is to these that the *Aṣṭāvakragītā* belongs, as is only to be expected from its clearly Vedāntin outlook. Unlike many such Gītās, the *Aṣṭāvakragītā* is not a mere reworking of the *Bhagavadgītā* and does not even quote directly from it, although there is little doubt that its author was well acquainted with the *Bhagavadgītā;* for example, echoes of BhG. 5.8–9 are probably seen in AG 17.8 + 12 and 18.47 + 65.

Occasionally, these independent Gītās are named after their supposed author rather than with a title indicating their sectarian affiliation. Two instances are the *Utathyagītā* and the *Vāmadevagītā,* both found in the *Mahābhārata* (at Mbh. 12.91–92 and 93–94). Similarly, Aṣṭāvakra first appears as the protagonist of the episode usually termed the *Aṣṭāvakrīya* but sometimes known as the *Aṣṭāvakragītā* (Mbh. 3.132–4), an episode which was probably inserted into the *Mahābhārata* during the course of its expansion but is nonetheless alluded to in the other epic, the *Rāmāyaṇa,* at a late point in its growth (Ram. 6.107.16). In this episode, Aṣṭāvakra, who appears as something of a child prodigy, at the age of twelve is able to defeat Janaka's *sūta* (bard or herald); Bandin, in riddling debate (probably a later form of the Vedic ritual *brahmodyas,* or contests about *brahman*). Although the numerical contest in which they engage (with each in turn composing a verse which lists concepts or entities characteristic of the numbers from one upward) is very different in form, its underlying concern with *brahman* is presumably the reason why Aṣṭāvakra was chosen as the expounder of the *Aṣṭāvakragītā;* if so, it is interesting that the *sūta* Bandin is replaced as the other main figure by Janaka, who is well known as one of the major debaters in the Upaniṣads.

This *Mahābhārata* episode interprets Aṣṭāvakra's name as meaning "crooked in eight ways" and explains it as resulting from his father's curse—rather obviously an etymological legend, a secondary explanation for an otherwise inexplicable name. The same mechanism of the curse is invoked in the story about Aṣṭāvakra found in the Purāṇas (ViP. 5.31.71–84 and Brahma P. 212.72–85), but this time Aṣṭāvakra curses the Apsaras who mock his deformity, which is much more in keeping with the popular view of ascetics as extremely irascible and liable to utter curses at the slightest provocation. Both stories are found together in later Sanskrit literature, for example the *Ayodhyāmāhātmya* (ed. Bakker, vol. 2, pp. 434–439). The same deformity and readiness to curse are found also in the modern Indian languages. In a story found in Adbhutācāryya's Bengali *Rāmāyaṇa* and the *svarga khaṇḍa* of the Bengali *Padmapurāṇa,* a mother takes advantage of both to make her son whole: she gives birth to a son, Bhagīratha, who is just a lump of flesh without bones, and following Vasiṣṭha's advice places him where he will see Aṣṭāvakra and, as anticipated, excite Aṣṭāvakra's wrath by his laughter which, since it is not ridiculing Aṣṭāvakra, leads in fact to his healing. In several versions of the *Manasāmaṅgal* of Bengal, Aṣṭāvakra curses Manasā's younger sister, Neto. In an Oriya work, the sixteenth-century *Śūnya Saṃhitā,* it is said that Aṣṭāvakra cursed the Yādavas "for some petty reason."

However, there is nothing in these later traditions about Aṣṭāvakra which is in any way helpful in understanding his role in the *Aṣṭāvakragītā* or why he was chosen to give a name to this essentially anonymous text. We are left with the significance of the context of the *Mahābhārata* episode as the only real clue. It is perhaps the relevance of that alone, combined with the similarity in title to the *Bhagavadgītā,* which has encouraged many Indian scholars to see it as belonging to the same period and thus as dating to around the fourth century B.C.E. They therefore see certain radical Advaitin views found in the *Aṣṭāvakragītā* which occur also in Gauḍapāda's writings as anticipating his ideas. In reality, however, the *Aṣṭāvakragītā* as a whole reveals a form of Advaita Vedānta which has undoubtedly undergone a long line of development and must at the least be later than Śaṃkara, the renowned codifier of the Advaita system. Doctrinally, the text has much in common with Sadānanda's *Vedāntasāra* and Vidyāraṇya's *Jīvanmuktiviveka* from the fourteenth and fifteenth centuries, while in its adaptation of an epic setting to the propagation of an Advaitin viewpoint it has analogies with the *Yogavāsiṣṭha,* a monumental twelfth- or thirteenth-century recasting of the *Rāmāyaṇa* as the basis for a passionate exposition of Advaita.

Gauḍapāda was the first exponent of Advaita Vedānta and traditionally is held to have been the teacher of Śaṃkara's teacher but more probably lived about three centuries earlier than Śaṃkara. Gauḍapāda's main doctrine was that of non-origination, according to which the whole world is merely an appearance: nothing ever really comes into being, since nothing other than *brahman* really exists, and the whole world is an illusion like a dream. Indeed, he goes so far as to declare that there is in principle no difference between waking and dreaming (*Māṇḍūkyakārikā* 2.4), thus abolishing a distinction on which Śaṃkara later insists. In the radicalism of his position on some points and in the evident similarities to Buddhist thought, Gauḍapāda exhibits a more extreme position than Śaṃkara and also than the *Aṣṭāvakragītā*.

Śaṃkara, as the founder of Advaita Vedānta and author of the *Brahmasūtrabhāṣya,* is the pivotal figure not only in philosophical views of the Advaita system, but also, to an extent often not sufficiently realized, in its organizational structure and hence its subsequent popularity. His central doctrine of the identity of *ātman* and *brahman,* of the individual self with the ground of the universe, is based on the Vedas, reconciling their apparent contradictions by recourse to the exegetical device of the two levels of truth, already well established in Buddhist thought. Much as Śaṃkara is admired as a philosopher, philosophy was not in fact his prime concern but the tool with which to achieve *mokṣa,* liberation, for himself and others. The multiple and finite entities of the phenomenal world are essentially identical with *brahman,* the Absolute, and it is only our ignorance or misunderstanding *(avidyā)* which prevents our seeing this. The multiplicity and individuality of phenomena lie in their separate identities which *avidyā* superimposes on the Absolute. When we perceive the world around us, we do perceive something but our mistake, our *avidyā,* consists in taking it as something other than *brahman;* this basic teaching Śaṃkara embodies repeatedly in illustrations, such as the rope and the snake or the silver and the mother-of-pearl, which have become part of the stock imagery of later Advaita.

For Śaṃkara the nature of *avidyā* is indescribable, since if it were entirely unreal we should not be entrapped by it and if it were real then *brahman* would not be the sole reality. Thus he denies the absolute reality of the world in order to affirm the sole reality of *brahman,* with which in its essential nature the *ātman* is identical. However, the individual self is a combination of reality and appearance—real insofar as it is *ātman* and thus *brahman,* but illusory insofar as it is limited and finite. *Brahman,* though, is not just an abstract concept but the goal of spiritual quest; release is achieved with the arrival of true knowledge, the realization that oneself and *brahman* are in truth identical. The awakening of this realization is therefore the overriding aim of all Śaṃkara's teaching. Later Advaita may sometimes become mainly scholastic (indeed, debate on the nature of *avidyā* and where it resides was to divide it into two subschools), but individual writers later were to present these ideas with all the fervor and persuasiveness of Śaṃkara himself.

At a later date a definite trend developed of using a somewhat more literary form as the vehicle for the teaching, often adopting the easy *śloka* metre of the Epics and Purāṇas as the medium and sometimes, as we have seen, even borrowing from the Epic narrative, in works like the *Yogavāsiṣṭha* and the *Adhyātma Rāmāyaṇa*. It is in this tradition that the *Aṣṭāvakragītā* stands and within which it is has achieved considerable popularity, not only in India but also in the West. The first translation into a European language was made as much as 120 years ago (an edition, published in 1868 at Florence, with Italian translation by Carlo Giussani); its author used three manuscripts from Tübingen and Petersburg. The more recent edition with German translation by Richard Hauschild is based on three manuscripts in Leipzig, as well as those by Giussani. Many other manuscripts exist in other European libraries, to say nothing of India. For example, there are as many as nine in the Bodleian Library, Oxford, including two which by their dates are older than any used by Giussani or Hauschild; however, a sample collation of these two demonstrates that there has been little variation in transmission of the text, though some in the titles given to the sections of the dialogue.

The text's significance for modern Vedāntins is well illustrated by the tradition that Vivekananda was introduced to the *Aṣṭāvakragītā* by Ramakrishna and valued the text. Its popularity is intimately connected with its character, for it is in many ways as much poetic as didactic, using the standard images of the Advaita system to excellent effect. It has with good reason been characterized as the outpourings of a realized individual. Certainly, its traditional form as a dialogue between Aṣṭāvakra as teacher and Janaka as pupil bears very little relationship to the message actually propounded. However, rather than trying to characterize the text any further, let me conclude and give the reader the opportunity of savoring it in this new and elegant translation by Dr. Byrom. There have been English translations before, but this is the first to capture the spirit of the original in its freshness and directness; I warmly recommend it.

J. L. Brockington
Department of Sanskrit
Edinburgh University

Acknowledgments

In 1980, with the help of the John Simon Guggenheim Foundation, I undertook a study of absurdism, which led me to an investigation of paradox in scriptural poetry, and finally to the present version of the *Ashtavakra Gita.* I wish to thank the Foundation for its support and encouragement.

For their scholarly guidance I wish to also thank Dr. Richard Gombrich, Professor of Sanskrit at Oxford University, who kindly clarified several difficult verses, and most especially Dr. John L. Brockington, Senior Lecturer in Sanskrit at Edinburgh University, who reviewed and emended my translation and my commentary at every turn with a generous patience.

Translator's Introduction: The Mystery of Awareness

I remember the moment clearly.

I had escaped from my sisters, over the rocks and around the point. I was barely seven. Above me, a rough escarpment of boulders singing in the midday heat, at my feet a rock pool of perfect, inviolable stillness, and beyond, the blue vastness of the South Pacific.

There was no other living creature. I was by myself, barefooted, between the cliff and the ocean.

As I squatted there, watching the reflection of the wind in the unrippled pool, hearing its exhilaration high above me in the bright emptiness of the sky, I became aware for the first time of awareness itself.

I had no name for it, but I could almost feel it, as if it had substance, like the water in the rock pool, or breath, like the shouting wind.

I saw that I was entirely by myself in a boundless ocean of awareness.

In the same instant I understood that awareness is the single mystery of life, that it enfolds all other mysteries, even the secret of the separate self.

From that moment I was indelibly astonished, and I knew that all my life I would be pinching myself and asking, *What is awareness?* Nothing else would ever command my attention so completely. How could it? For nothing else mattered next to the constant pressure, the single compulsion of this mystery.

A quarter of a century went by, and one day my teacher placed in my hands a copy of Mukerjee's edition of the *Ashtavakra Gita.* I had by then, in the ordinary course of my seeking, read a great deal of scripture, enough to know the truth of Ashtavakra's admonition, halfway through his own Song: "My child, you can talk about holy books all you like. But until you forget everything, you will never find yourself." Understanding the vanity of scripture, I hardly expected Ashtavakra to solve in a single epiphany the mystery of awareness.

And yet, as I read his spare and simple verses, I felt that here at last were words which in some measure consumed my astonishment. They spoke so directly, and so modestly. They seemed so austere, and yet so generous. I found myself once more a child of seven, tipped between the sea and the sky, but hearing now in the wind's exuberance a clearer music, touching the heart of the mystery.

"What is the rising or the vanishing of thought? What is the visible world, or the invisible? What is the little soul, or God Himself?"

Awareness. Pure awareness. The clear space, the sky, the heart of awareness.

Ashtavakra's words begin after almost everything else has been said. They barely touch the page. They are often on the point of vanishing. They are the first melting of the snow, high in the mountains, a clear stream flowing over smooth and shining pebbles. Theirs is the radiance of the winter sky above Trishul, Kailash, Annapurna. My *satguru,* Neem Karoli Baba, called the *Ashtavakra Gita* "the purest of scriptures." All its beauty is in the transparency, its enraptured and flawless purity.

It is written as a dialogue between King Janaka, the father of Sita, and his guru, Ashtavakra. But this is just a literary device, unsupported by any internal drama, and I have done away with it in my version. The Gita has only one voice, Ashtavakra's, a voice of singular compassion and uncompromised clarity.

He is not concerned to argue. This is not speculative philosophy. It is a kind of knowledge. Ashtavakra speaks as a man who has already found his way and now wishes to share it. His song is a direct and practical transcript of experience, a radical account of ineffable truths.

He speaks, moreover, in a language that is for all its modesty physical and direct. He is not abstract, though some translations, laboring to render his special terms faithfully, make him sound difficult, even abstruse.

On the contrary, Ashtavakra is very simple.

We are all one Self. The Self is pure awareness. This Self, this flawless awareness is God. There is only God.

Everything else is an illusion: the little self, the world, the universe. All these things arise with the thought "I," that is, with the idea of separate identity. The little "I" invents the material world, which in our ignorance we strive hard to sustain. Forgetting our original oneness, bound tightly in our imaginary separateness, we spend our lives mastered by a specious sense of purpose and value. Endlessly constrained by our habit of individuation, the creature of preference and desire, we continually set one thing against another, until the mischief and misery of choice consume us.

But our true nature is pure and choiceless awareness. We are already and always fulfilled. "It is easy," says Ashtavakra. "You are the clear space of awareness *(cidākāśa),* pure and still, in whom there is no birth, no striving, no 'I'."

Then how do we recover our original awareness? How do we dispel the illusion of separation?

Some commentators suppose that Ashtavakra is really not concerned to answer these questions. For them, his Gita is a transcendent confession too pure to be useful. Others see it as earnestly didactic, a manual of conduct. Both are right. Ashtavakra is indeed wild, playful, utterly absorbed in the Self. Since words are of the mind, which arises only to obscure awareness, words are indeed folly. And who would teach folly?

Ashtavakra would. His is an eminently compassionate and practical madness. Even while cutting the ground from under our feet, he shows us at every turn what to do. With a crazy solicitude, he tells us how to end our Self-estrangement.

Be happy. Love yourself. Don't judge others. Forgive. Always be simple. Don't make distinctions. Give up the habit of choice. Let the mind dissolve. Give up preferring and desiring. Desire only your own awareness. Give up identifying with the body and the senses. Give up your attachment to meditation and service. Give up your attachment to detachment.

Give up giving up! Reject nothing, accept nothing. Be still. But above all, be happy. In the end, you will find yourself "just by knowing how things are."

It would be perverse and humorless to suppose that just because Ashtavakra, with his irreducible nondualism, considers meditation merely a distracting habit, he means us to abandon our practice. Of course, from the perspective of unconditional freedom, where nothing makes any difference, meditation seems a comically self-important waste of time. But Ashtavakra makes it plain. "The moment a fool gives up his spiritual practices, he falls prey to fancies and desires." God help the seeker who presumes that since he is already and always fulfilled, he can give up trying.

It is all a matter of knowing. We are all indeed already perfect, but until we know it, we had better deal with our ignorance, and that can't be done just by listening to words. It requires *sādhana,* trying, doing what we do not wish to do. It means long, hard, self-effacing work.

The heart of Ashtavakra's advice is not to give up our practice, but to abandon our strenuous indolence. "Striving is the root of sorrow," he says. "But who understands this?" Look at the master, he says. Who is lazier? He has trouble even blinking! He certainly does not run around puffing himself up looking for God or liberation, busily making excuses for not finding himself.

Dealing with our ignorance also means, for almost all of us, finding someone like Ashtavakra to help us. We cannot easily break the spell ourselves. Here again, Ashtavakra is very practical. At least half of the book describes the nature of the master, the man who has found his way.

It is an austere and enchanting portrait. The master is a child, a fool, a man asleep, a leaf tumbling in the wind. Inside he is utterly free. He does exactly as he pleases. Rules mean nothing to him. He doesn't care who makes fun of him, because he is always playing and having a wonderful time. He lives as if he had no body. He seems to walk on air. He is unsmudged, like the clear sky or the smooth and shining surface of a vast lake.

Because we are subject to the dualities which he has transcended, we glimpse his nature only through paradox. He sees but he sees nothing. He sees what cannot be seen. He knows but he knows nothing. He sleeps soundly without sleeping. He dreams without dreaming. He is busy but he does nothing. He is not alive, nor is he dead.

His secret, and the ultimate paradox, is that he stands on his own. He is completely by himself (*svāsthya*). Only by an absolute independence (*svātantrya*) has he discovered his absolute oneness with all things.

Who was this Ashtavakra, this uncompromising poet and saint?

Since Ashtavakra's whole point is that individual identity is an illusion, it is a perfect irony that the only certain thing we can say about him is that he was not Ashtavakra. He was an anonymous master who adopted Ashtavakra's character as he found it represented in a number of tales in classical Indian literature, and used it as a suitably faceless mask through which to deliver his gospel of self-effacement.

The best known tale, in the *Mahābhārata,* explains how he got his name, which means "eight twists." When still in his mother's womb, Ashtavakra overheard his father Kahoda reciting the Vedas. Though still unborn he already knew the scriptures, and hearing his father's mistakes, he called out to correct him. Kahoda was insulted and cursed him, and in due course he was born with deformed limbs.

Some years later, at the court of Janaka, Kahoda engaged in a debate with the great scholar Bandin, son of King Varuna. He was defeated, and Bandin had him drowned.

When Ashtavakra was twelve he discovered what had happened. He went at once to Janaka's court where he beat Bandin in debate. Bandin then explained that his father had not been drowned, but had been banished to the bottom of the sea to serve King Varuna. He released Kahoda, who wished at once to lift the curse from his son. He told Ashtavakra to bathe in the river Samanga. When he came out of the water, his body was straight.

There is another story about him in the *Vishnu Purāṇa.* As Ashtavakra was performing penances under water, celestial nymphs gathered and sang for him. He was so delighted, he gave them a boon: they would all marry Krishna. But when he came out of the water, the nymphs saw his deformities and made fun of him. Ashtavakra added a curse to the boon: after their marriage they would all fall into the hands of robbers. And so it happened. They all married Krishna, but after his death, despite the efforts of Arjuna, they were all carried off by robbers.

The moral of both stories* is, of course, that even the ugliest form is filled with God's radiance. The body is nothing, the Self is everything. There may be, as well, some notion of the sacrificial value of deformity, of the kind we find in Saint Augustine when he remarks of the breaking of Christ's body on the cross "his deformity forms you."

So the *Ashtavakra Gita* was written by an unknown master who took his inspiration from the contest between Ashtavakra and Bandin, which Ashtavakra wins by demonstrating the absolute oneness of

---

*See also *Śathapatha Brāhmaṇa* 11.6.2; *Rāmāyaṇa* 6.107.16; *Brahma Purāṇa* 212.71–92.

God *(brahmadvaitam)*. Though he casts his verses as a debate, there is, as I have said, no real dialogue. Only one voice is heard, speaking through the assumed character and with the borrowed yet potent authority and special facelessness of Ashtavakra. And it is entirely appropriate that the real master of the Gita remain forever unknown since, as he has Ashtavakra say of himself, "for what he has become there is no name."

We not only know next to nothing about him, we cannot even be sure when he lived. Sanskrit was so static, especially after Panini's account of it became prescriptive, a little before Christ, that its literature is hard to date on linguistic evidence alone. Since we have only the slimmest literary, historical, or philosophical evidence besides, it is very hard to date the *Ashtavakra Gita* with any accuracy. Indian editors usually argue, with some sentimentality, that it was written in the same age as or just before the *Bhagavad Gita,* which they date to the fifth or fourth century B.C.E. Western editors not only place the *Bhagavad Gita* much later, probably in the first or second century C.E., but they generally agree that the *Ashtavakra Gita* comes a good deal later still. Without rehearsing the arguments, we may safely guess that it was written either in the eighth century by a follower of Shankara, or in the fourteenth century during a resurgence of Shankara's teaching. As a distillation of monistic Vedanta, it certainly has all the marks of Shankara's purification of ancient Shaivism.

Ashtavakra ends his Gita with a litany of self-dismissive questions, all of them utterly rhetorical. "What is good or evil? Life or death? Freedom or bondage? Illusion or the world? Creation or dissolution? The Self or the not-Self?" The Sanskrit literally asks "where?" rather than "what?" "Where is the little soul, or God Himself?" Within the ever-fulfilled and ubiquitous Self there is no place for these—or any—distinctions.

There is no place even for spiritual enquiry. "Who is the seeker?" Ashtavakra asks. "What has he found? What is seeking or the end of seeking?" These final questions dissolve even the voice which asks them. "Who is the disciple, and who the master?" With this last gesture of self-erasure, the nameless master is finally free to declare his real identity, which he shares unconditionally with all beings.

> For I have no bounds.
>
> I am Shiva.
>
> Nothing arises in me.
> In whom nothing is single,
> Nothing is double.
>
> Nothing is,
> Nothing is not.
>
> What more is there to say?

Some years ago, when we first settled in our ashram in Florida, we used to go out riding in the very early morning. My teacher always insisted that we take with us a much-thumbed, broken-backed but well-loved copy of the *Ashtavakra Gita.* We would saddle our horses before dawn and ride out along the banks of the Sebastian River. I remember the frost glazing the water, the ghostly breath of the horses, and on the western horizon the thin crescent of a Shiva moon. Once, looking back when the horses shied, I saw a panther standing in our tracks, silent and unafraid, smelling our voices.

Just before the sun came up we would dismount and, gathering frosted palm fans and handfuls of oak duff, make a fire. And as the sun rose above the bright water we read aloud from the Gita.

> It is easy.
>
> God made all things.
> There is only God.

When you know this
Desire melts away.

Clinging to nothing,
You become still . . .

Thomas Byrom
Kashi Foundation
July 1989

1 *The Self*

1 O Master,
Tell me how to find
Detachment, wisdom, and freedom!

2 Child,
If you wish to be free,
Shun the poison of the senses.

Seek the nectar of truth,
Of love and forgiveness,
Simplicity and happiness.

3 Earth, fire and water,
The wind and the sky—
You are none of these.

If you wish to be free,
Know you are the Self,
The witness of all these,
The heart of awareness.

4 Set your body aside.
Sit in your own awareness.

You will at once be happy,
Forever still,
Forever free.

5 You have no caste.
No duties bind you.

Formless and free,
Beyond the reach of the senses,
The witness of all things.

So be happy!

6 Right or wrong,
Joy and sorrow,
These are of the mind only.
They are not yours.

It is not really you
Who acts or enjoys.

You are everywhere,
Forever free.

7 Forever and truly free,
The single witness of all things.

But if you see yourself as separate,
Then you are bound.

8 "I do this. I do that."
The big black snake of selfishness
Has bitten you!

"I do nothing."
This is the nectar of faith,
So drink and be happy!

9 Know you are one,
Pure awareness.

With the fire of this conviction,
Burn down the forest of ignorance.

Free yourself from sorrow,
And be happy.

10 Be happy!
For you are joy, unbounded joy.

You are awareness itself.

Just as a coil of rope
Is mistaken for a snake,
So you are mistaken for the world.

11 If you think you are free,
You are free.

If you think you are bound,
You are bound.

For the saying is true:
You are what you think.

12 The Self looks like the world.
But this is just an illusion.

The Self is everywhere.

One.
Still.
Free.
Perfect.

The witness of all things,
Awareness
Without action, clinging or desire.

13 Meditate on the Self.
One without two,
Exalted awareness.

Give up the illusion
Of the separate self.

Give up the feeling,
Within or without,
That you are this or that.

14 My Child,
Because you think you are the body,
For a long time you have been bound.

Know you are pure awareness.

With this knowledge as your sword
Cut through your chains.

And be happy!

15 For you are already free,
Without action or flaw,
Luminous and bright.

You are bound
Only by the habit of meditation.

16 Your nature is pure awareness.

You are flowing in all things,
And all things are flowing in you.

But beware
The narrowness of the mind!

17 You are always the same,
Unfathomable awareness,
Limitless and free,
Serene and unperturbed.

Desire only your own awareness.

18 Whatever takes form is false.
Only the formless endures.

When you understand
The truth of this teaching,
You will not be born again.

19 For God is infinite,
Within the body and without,
Like a mirror,
And the image in a mirror.

20 As the air is everywhere,
Flowing around a pot
And filling it,
So God is everywhere,
Filling all things
And flowing through them forever.

2 *Awareness*

1 Yesterday
I lived bewildered,
In illusion.

But now I am awake,
Flawless and serene,
Beyond the world.

2 From my light
The body and the world arise.

So all things are mine,
Or nothing is.

3 Now I have given up
The body and the world,
I have a special gift.

I see the infinite Self.

4 As a wave,
Seething and foaming,
Is only water

So all creation,
Streaming out of the Self,
Is only the Self.

5 Consider a piece of cloth.
It is only threads!

So all creation,
When you look closely,
Is only the Self.

6 Like the sugar
In the juice of the sugarcane,
I am the sweetness
In everything I have made.

7 When the Self is unknown
The world arises,
Not when it is known.

But you mistake
The rope for the snake.

When you see the rope,
The snake vanishes.

8 My nature is light,
Nothing but light.

When the world arises
I alone am shining.

9 When the world arises in me,
It is just an illusion:
Water shimmering in the sun,
A vein of silver in mother-of-pearl,
A serpent in a strand of rope.

10 From me the world streams out
And in me it dissolves,
As a bracelet melts into gold,
A pot crumbles into clay,
A wave subsides into water.

11 I adore myself.
How wonderful I am!

I can never die.

The whole world may perish,
From Brahma to a blade of grass,
But I am still here.

12 Indeed how wonderful!
I adore myself.

For I have taken form
But I am still one.

Neither coming or going,
Yet I am still everywhere.

13 How wonderful,
And how great my powers!

For I am without form,
Yet till the end of time
I uphold the universe.

14 Wonderful!

For nothing is mine,
Yet it is all mine,
Whatever is thought or spoken.

15 I am not the knower,
Nor the known,
Nor the knowing.

These three are not real.
They only seem to be
When I am not known.

For I am flawless.

16 Two from one!
This is the root of suffering.

Only perceive
That I am one without two,
Pure awareness, pure joy,
And all the world is false.

There is no other remedy!

17 Through ignorance
I once imagined I was bound.

But I am pure awareness.

I live beyond all distinctions,
In unbroken meditation.

18 Indeed,
I am neither bound nor free.

An end to illusion!
It is all groundless.

For the whole of creation,
Though it rests in me,
Is without foundation.

19 The body is nothing.
The world is nothing.

When you understand this fully,
How can they be invented?

For the Self is pure awareness,
Nothing less.

20 The body is false,
And so are its fears,
Heaven and hell, freedom and bondage.

It is all invention.

What can they matter to me?

I am awareness itself.

21 I see only one.

Many men,
One wilderness.

Then to what may I cling?

22 I am not the body.
Nor is the body mine.

I am not separate.

I am awareness itself,
Bound only by my thirst for life.

23 I am the infinite ocean.

When thoughts spring up,
The wind freshens, and like waves
A thousand worlds arise.

24 But when the wind falls,
The trader sinks with his ship.

On the boundless ocean of my being
He founders,
And all the worlds with him.

25 But O how wonderful!

I am the unbounded deep
In whom all living things
Naturally arise,
Rush against each other playfully,
And then subside.

3 *Wisdom*

1 You know the Self,
By nature one
Without end.

You know the Self,
And you are serene.

How can you still desire riches?

2 When from ignorance
You see silver in mother-of-pearl,
Greed arises.

From ignorance of the Self
Desire arises
For the world where the senses whirl.

3 Knowing yourself as That
In which the worlds rise and fall
Like waves in the ocean,
Why do you run about so wretchedly?

4 For have you not heard?

You are pure awareness,
And your beauty is infinite!

So why let lust mislead you?

5 The man who is wise
Knows himself in all things
And all things in himself.

Yet how strange!
He still says, "This is mine."

6 Determined to be free,
He abides in the oneness
Beyond all things.

Yet how strange!
Indulging in passion, he weakens,
And lust overwhelms him.

7 Feeble with age,
Still he is filled with desire,
When without doubt he knows
That lust is the enemy of awareness.

Indeed how strange!

8 He longs to be free . . .

He has no care for this world
Or the next,
And he knows what is passing
Or forever.

And yet how strange!
He is still afraid of freedom.

9 But he who is truly wise
Always sees the absolute Self.

Celebrated, he is not delighted.
Spurned, he is not angry.

10 Pure of heart,
He watches his own actions
As if they were another's.

How can praise or blame disturb him?

11 With clear and steady insight
He sees this world is a mirage,
And he no longer wonders about it.

How can he fear the approach of death?

12 Pure of heart,
He desires nothing,
Even in despair.

He is content
In the knowledge of the Self.

With whom may I compare him?

13 With clear and steady insight
He knows that whatever he sees
Is by its very nature nothing.

How can he prefer one thing to another?

14 He is beyond all duality.

Free from desire,
He has driven from his mind
All longing for the world.

Come what may,
Joy or sorrow,
Nothing moves him.

4 *The True Seeker*

1 The wise man knows the Self,
And he plays the game of life.

But the fool lives in the world
Like a beast of burden.

2 The true seeker feels no elation,
Even in that exalted state
Which Indra and all the gods
Unhappily long for.

3 He understands the nature of things.

His heart is not smudged
By right or wrong,
As the sky is not smudged by smoke.

4 He is pure of heart,
He knows the whole world is only the Self.

So who can stop him
From doing as he wishes?

5 Of the four kinds of being,
From Brahma to a blade of grass,
Only the wise man is strong enough
To give up desire and aversion.

6 How rare he is!

Knowing he is the Self,
He acts accordingly
And is never fearful.

For he knows he is the Self,
One without two,
The Lord of all creation.

5 *Dissolving*

1 You are pure.
Nothing touches you.
What is there to renounce?

Let it all go,
The body and the mind.

Let yourself dissolve.

2 Like bubbles in the sea,
All the worlds arise in you.

Know you are the Self.
Know you are one.

Let yourself dissolve.

3 You see the world.
But like the snake in the rope,
It is not really there.

You are pure.

Let yourself dissolve.

4 You are one and the same
In joy and sorrow,
Hope and despair,
Life and death.

You are already fulfilled.

Let yourself dissolve.

6 *Knowledge*

1 I am boundless space.
The world is a clay pot.

This is the truth.

There is nothing to accept,
Nothing to reject,
Nothing to dissolve.

2 I am the ocean.
All the worlds are like waves.

This is the truth.

Nothing to hold on to,
Nothing to let go of,
Nothing to dissolve.

3 I am the mother-of-pearl.
The world is a vein of silver,
An illusion!

This is the truth.

Nothing to grasp,
Nothing to spurn,
Nothing to dissolve.

4 I am in all beings.
All beings are in me.

This is the whole truth.

Nothing to embrace,
Nothing to relinquish,
Nothing to dissolve.

7 *The Boundless Ocean*

1 I am the boundless ocean.

This way and that,
The wind, blowing where it will,
Drives the ship of the world.

But I am not shaken.

2 I am the unbounded deep
In whom the waves of all the worlds
Naturally rise and fall.

But I do not rise or fall.

3 I am the infinite deep
In whom all the worlds
Appear to rise.

Beyond all form,
Forever still.

Even so am I.

4 I am not in the world.
The world is not in me.

I am pure.
I am unbounded.

Free from attachment,
Free from desire,
Still.

Even so am I.

O how wonderful!

I am awareness itself,
No less.

The world is a magic show!

But in me
There is nothing to embrace,
And nothing to turn away.

8 The Mind

1 The mind desires this,
And grieves for that.
It embraces one thing,
And spurns another.

Now it feels anger,
Now happiness.

In this way you are bound.

2 But when the mind desires nothing
And grieves for nothing,
When it is without joy or anger
And, grasping nothing,
Turns nothing away . . .

Then you are free.

3 When the mind is attracted
To anything it senses,
You are bound.

When there is no attraction,
You are free.

4 Where there is no I,
You are free.

Where there is I,
You are bound.

Consider this.

It is easy.

Embrace nothing,
Turn nothing away.

9 *Dispassion*

1 Seeing to this,
Neglecting that,
Setting one thing against another . . .

Who is free of such cares?
When will they ever end?

Consider.

Without passion,
With dispassion,
Let go.

2 My Child,
Rare is he, and blessed,
Who observes the ways of men
And gives up the desire
For pleasure and knowledge,
For life itself.

3 Nothing lasts.
Nothing is real.

It is all suffering,
Threefold affliction!
It is all beneath contempt.

Know this.
Give it up.
Be still.

4 When will men ever stop
Setting one thing against another?

Let go of all contraries.
Whatever comes, be happy
And so fulfill yourself.

5 Masters, saints, seekers:
They all say different things.

Whoever knows this,
With dispassion becomes quiet.

6 The true master considers well.
With dispassion
He sees all things are the same.

He comes to understand
The nature of things,
The essence of awareness.

He will not be born again.

7 In the shifting elements
See only their pure form.

Rest in your own nature.
Set yourself free.

8 The world is just a set of false impressions.
Give them up.

Give up the illusion.
Give up the world.

And live freely.

10 Desire

1 Striving and craving,
For pleasure or prosperity,
These are your enemies,
Springing up to destroy you
From the presumptions of virtue.

Let them all go.
Hold on to nothing.

2 Every good fortune,
Wives, friends, houses, lands,
All these gifts and riches . . .

They are a dream,
A juggling act,
A traveling show!

A few days, and they are gone.

3 Consider.

Wherever there is desire,
There is the world.

With resolute dispassion
Free yourself from desire,
And find happiness.

4 Desire binds you,
Nothing else.
Destroy it, and you are free.

Turn from the world.
Fulfill yourself,
And find lasting happiness.

5 You are one.
You are pure awareness.

The world is not real.
It is cold and lifeless.

Nor is ignorance real.
So what can you wish to know?

6 Life after life you indulged
In different forms,
Different pleasures,
Sons and kingdoms and wives.

Only to lose them all . . .

7 Enough of the pursuit of pleasure,
Enough of wealth and righteous deeds!

In the dark forest of the world
What peace of mind can they bring you?

8 How you have toiled,
Life after life,
Pressing into painful labor
Your body and your mind and your words.

It is time to stop.

Now!

11 Stillness

1 All things arise,
Suffer change,
And pass away.

This is their nature.

When you know this,
Nothing perturbs you,
Nothing hurts you.

You become still.

It is easy.

2 God made all things.
There is only God.

When you know this,
Desire melts away.

Clinging to nothing,
You become still.

3 Sooner or later,
Fortune or misfortune
May befall you.

When you know this,
You desire nothing,
You grieve for nothing.

Subduing the senses,
You are happy.

4 Whatever you do
Brings joy or sorrow,
Life or death.

When you know this,
You may act freely,
Without attachment.

For what is there to accomplish?

5 All sorrow comes from fear.
From nothing else.

When you know this,
You become free of it,
And desire melts away.

You become happy
And still.

6 "I am not the body,
Nor is the body mine.
I am awareness itself."

When you know this,
You have no thought
For what you have done
Or left undone.

You become one,
Perfect and indivisible.

7 "I am in all things,
From Brahma to a blade of grass."

When you know this,
You have no thought
For success or failure
Or the mind's inconstancy.

You are pure.
You are still.

8 The world with all its wonders
Is nothing.

When you know this,
Desire melts away.

For you are awareness itself.

When you know in your heart
That there is nothing,
You are still.

12 *Fulfillment*

1 First I gave up action,
Then idle words,
And lastly thought itself.

Now I am here.

2 Ridding my mind of distraction,
Single-pointed,
I shut out sound and all the senses,
And I am here.

3 Meditation is needed
Only when the mind is distracted
By false imagining.

Knowing this,
I am here.

4 Without joy or sorrow,
Grasping nothing, spurning nothing,
O Master, I am here.

5 What do I care
If I observe or neglect
The four stages of life?

Meditation,
Controlling the mind,
These are mere distractions!

Now I am here.

6 Doing, or not doing,
Both come from not knowing.

Knowing this fully,
I am here.

7 Thinking
Of what is beyond thinking
Is still thinking.

I gave up thinking,
And I am here.

8 Whoever fulfills this
Fulfills his own nature
And is indeed fulfilled.

13 Happiness

1 Even if you have nothing,
It is hard to find that contentment
Which comes from renunciation.

I accept nothing.
I reject nothing.

And I am happy.

2 The body trembles,
The tongue falters,
The mind is weary.

Forsaking them all,
I pursue my purpose happily.

3 Knowing I do nothing,
I do whatever comes my way,
And I am happy.

4 Bound to his body,
The seeker insists on striving
Or on sitting still.

But I no longer suppose
The body is mine,
Or is not mine.

And I am happy.

5 Sleeping, sitting, walking,
Nothing good or bad befalls me.

I sleep, I sit, I walk,
And I am happy.

6 Struggling or at rest,
Nothing is won or lost.

I have forsaken the joy of winning
And the sorrow of losing.

And I am happy.

7 For pleasures come and go.
How often I have watched their inconstancy!

But I have forsaken good and bad,
And now I am happy.

14 The Fool

1 By nature my mind is empty.
Even in sleep, I am awake.
I think of things without thinking.

All my impressions of the world
Have dissolved.

2 My desires have melted away.

So what do I care for money
Or the thieving senses,
For friends or knowledge or holy books?

3 Liberation,
Bondage,
What are they to me?

What do I care for freedom?

For I have known God,
The infinite Self,
The witness of all things.

4 Without, a fool.
Within, free of thought.

I do as I please,
And only those like me
Understand my ways.

15 *The Clear Space of Awareness*

1 The man who is pure of heart
Is bound to fulfill himself
In whatever way he is taught.

A worldly man seeks all his life,
But is still bewildered.

2 Detached from the senses,
You are free.

Attached, you are bound.

When this is understood,
You may live as you please.

3 When this is understood,
The man who is bright and busy
And full of fine words
Falls silent.

He does nothing.
He is still.

No wonder
Those who wish to enjoy the world
Shun this understanding!

4 You are not your body.
Your body is not you.

You are not the doer.
You are not the enjoyer.

You are pure awareness,
The witness of all things.

You are without expectation,
Free.

Wherever you go,
Be happy!

5 Desire and aversion are of the mind.
The mind is never yours.
You are free of its turmoil.

You are awareness itself,
Never changing.

Wherever you go,
Be happy.

6 For see!
The Self is in all beings,
And all beings are in the Self.

Know you are free,
Free of "I,"
Free of "mine."

Be happy.

7 In you the worlds arise
Like waves in the sea.

It is true!
You are awareness itself.

So free yourself
From the fever of the world.

8 Have faith, my Child, have faith.

Do not be bewildered.

For you are beyond all things,
The heart of all knowing.

You are the Self.
You are God.

9 The body is confined
By its natural properties.

It comes,
It lingers awhile,
It goes.

But the Self neither comes nor goes.
So why grieve for the body?

10 If the body lasted till the end of time,
Or vanished today,
What would you win or lose?

You are pure awareness.

11 You are the endless sea
In whom all the worlds like waves
Naturally rise and fall.

You have nothing to win,
Nothing to lose.

12 Child,
You are pure awareness,
Nothing less.

You and the world are one.

So who are you to think
You can hold on to it,
Or let it go?

How could you!

13 You are the clear space of awareness,
Pure and still,
In whom there is no birth,
No activity,
No "I."

You are one and the same.
You cannot change or die.

14 You are in whatever you see.
You alone.

Just as bracelets and bangles
And dancing anklets
Are all of the same gold.

15 "I am not this."
"I am He."
Give up such distinctions.

Know that everything is the Self.
Rid yourself of all purpose.

And be happy.

16 The world only arises from ignorance.
You alone are real.

There is no one,
Not even God,
Separate from yourself.

17 You are pure awareness.

The world is an illusion,
Nothing more.

When you understand this fully,
Desire falls away.

You find peace.

For indeed!
There is nothing.

18 In the ocean of being
There is only one.

There was and there will be
Only one.

You are already fulfilled.
How can you be bound or free?

Wherever you go,
Be happy.

19 Never upset your mind
With yes and no.

Be quiet.
You are awareness itself.

Live in the happiness
Of your own nature,
Which is happiness itself.

20 What is the use of thinking?

Once and for all,
Give up meditation.
Hold nothing in your mind.

You are the Self,
And you are free.

16 *Forget Everything*

1 My Child,
You may read or discuss scripture
As much as you like.

But until you forget everything,
You will never live in your heart.

2 You are wise.
You play and work and meditate.

But still your mind desires
That which is beyond everything,
Where all desires vanish.

3 Striving is the root of sorrow.

But who understands this?

Only when you are blessed
With the understanding of this teaching
Will you find freedom.

4 Who is lazier than the master?
He has trouble even blinking!

But only he is happy.
No one else!

5 Seeing to this,
Neglecting that . . .

But when the mind stops setting
One thing against another,
It no longer craves pleasure.

It no longer cares for wealth
Or religious duties or salvation.

6 Craving the pleasures of the senses,
You suffer attachment.

Disdaining them,
You learn detachment.

But if you desire nothing,
And disdain nothing,
Neither attachment nor detachment bind you.

7 When you live without discrimination,
Desire arises.

When desire persists,
Feelings of preference arise,
Of liking and disliking.

They are the root and branches of the world.

8 From activity, desire.
From renunciation, aversion.

But the man of wisdom is a child.
He never sets one thing against another.

It is true!
He is a child.

9 If you desire the world,
You may try to renounce it
In order to escape sorrow.

Instead, renounce desire!
Then you will be free of sorrow,
And the world will not trouble you.

10 If you desire liberation,
But you still say "mine,"
If you feel you are the body,
You are not a wise man or a seeker.

You are simply a man who suffers.

11 Let Hari teach you,
Or Brahma, born of the lotus,
Or Shiva Himself!

Unless you forget everything,
You will never live in your heart.

17 Beyond All

1 The man who is happy and pure
And likes his own company
Gathers the fruit of his practice
And the fruit of wisdom.

2 The man who knows the truth
Is never unhappy in the world.

For he alone fills the universe.

3 Just as the elephant loves
The leaves of the sallaki tree,
But not the neem tree,
So the man who loves himself
Always spurns the senses.

4 It is hard to find
A man who has no desire
For what he has not tasted,
Or who tastes the world
And is untouched.

5 Here in the world
Some crave pleasure,
Some seek freedom.

But it is hard to find
A man who wants neither.

He is a great soul.

6 It is hard to find
A man who has an open mind,
Who neither seeks nor shuns
Wealth or pleasure,
Duty or liberation,
Life or death . . .

7 He does not want the world to end.
He does not mind if it lasts.

Whatever befalls him,
He lives in happiness.

For he is truly blessed.

8 Now that he understands,
He is fulfilled.
His mind is drawn within,
And he is fulfilled.

He sees and he hears,
He touches and smells and tastes,
And he is happy.

9 Whatever he does is without purpose.
His senses have been stilled.
His eyes are empty.

He is without desire or aversion.

For him the waters of the world
Have all dried up!

10 He is not asleep.
He is not awake.
He never closes his eyes
Or opens them.

Wherever he is,
He is beyond everything.
He is free.

11 And the man who is free
Always lives in his heart.
His heart is always pure.

Whatever happens,
He is free of all desires.

12 Whatever he sees or hears or touches,
Whatever he smells or tastes,
Whatever he acquires,
He is free.

Free from striving,
And from stillness.

For indeed he is a great soul.

13 Without blame or praise,
Anger or rejoicing.

He gives nothing.
He takes nothing.

He wants nothing,
Nothing at all.

14 And whoever draws near him,
A woman full of passion
Or Death Himself,
He is not shaken.

He stays in his heart.

He is free indeed!

15 It is all the same to him.
Man or woman,
Good fortune or bad,
Happiness or sorrow.

It makes no difference.
He is serene.

16 The world no longer holds him.
He has gone beyond
The bounds of human nature.

Without compassion
Or the wish to harm,
Without pride or humility.

Nothing disturbs him.
Nothing surprises him.

17 Because he is free,
He neither craves nor disdains
The things of the world.

He takes them as they come.

His mind is always detached.

18 His mind is empty.
He is not concerned with meditation,
Or the absence of it,
Or the struggle between good and evil.

He is beyond all,
Alone.

19 No "I,"
No "mine."

He knows there is nothing.

All his inner desires have melted away.

Whatever he does,
He does nothing.

20 His mind has stopped working!

It has simply melted away . . .

And with it,
Dreams and delusions and dullness.

And for what he has become,
There is no name.

18 The Master

1 Love your true Self,
Which is naturally happy
And peaceful and bright!

Awaken to your own nature,
And all delusion melts like a dream.

2 How much pleasure you take
In acquiring worldly goods!

But to find happiness
You must give them all up.

3 The sorrows of duty,
Like the heat of the sun,
Have scorched your heart.

But let stillness fall on you
With its sweet and cooling showers,
And you will find happiness.

4 For the world is nothing.
It is only an idea.

But the essence of what is
And of what is not
Can never fail.

5 The Self is always the same,
Already fulfilled,
Without flaw or choice or striving.

Close at hand,
But boundless.

6 When the Self is known,
All illusions vanish.

The veil falls,
And you see clearly.

Your sorrows are dispelled.

7 For the Self is free
And lives forever.

Everything else is imagination,
Nothing more!

Because he understands this,
The master acts like a child.

8 When you know you are God
And that what is and what is not
Are both imaginary,
And you are at last free of desire,
Then what is there left
To know or to say or to do?

9 For the Self is everything.

When the seeker knows this,
He falls silent.

He no longer thinks,
"I am this, I am not that."

Such thoughts melt away.

10 He is still.

Without pleasure or pain,
Distraction or concentration,
Learning or ignorance.

11 His nature is free of conditions.

Win or lose,
It makes no difference to him.

Alone in the forest or out in the world,
A god in heaven or a simple beggar,
It makes no difference!

12 He is free of duality.

Wealth or pleasure,
Duty or discrimination
Mean nothing to him.

What does he care
What is accomplished or neglected?

13 Finding freedom in this life,
The seeker takes nothing to heart,
Neither duty nor desire.

He has nothing to do
But to live out his life.

14 The master lives beyond the boundaries of desire.

Delusion or the world,
Meditation on the truth,
Liberation itself—
What are they to him?

15 You see the world
And you try to dissolve it.

But the master has no need to.
He is without desire.

For though he sees,
He sees nothing.

16 When you have seen God
You meditate on Him,
Saying to yourself, "I am He."

But when you are without thought
And you understand there is only one,
Without a second,
On whom can you meditate?

17 When you are distracted,
You practice concentration.

But the master is undistracted.

He has nothing to fulfill.
What is there left for him to accomplish?

18 He acts like an ordinary man.
But inside he is quite different.

He sees no imperfection in himself,
Nor distraction,
Nor any need for meditation.

19 He is awake,
Fulfilled,
Free from desire.

He neither is nor is not.

He looks busy,
But he does nothing.

20 Striving or still,
He is never troubled.

He does whatever comes his way,
And he is happy.

21 He has no desires.
He has cast off his chains.
He walks on air.

He is free,
Tumbling like a leaf in the wind,
From life to life.

22 He has gone beyond the world,
Beyond joy and sorrow.

His mind is always cool.
He lives as if he had no body.

23 His mind is cool and pure.
He delights in the Self.

There is nothing he wishes to renounce.
He misses nothing.

24 His mind is naturally empty.
He does as he pleases.

He is not an ordinary man.
Honor and dishonor mean nothing to him.

25 "The body does this, not I."
"My nature is purity."

With these thoughts,
Whatever he does,
He does nothing.

26 But he pretends not to know.

He finds freedom in this life,
But he acts like an ordinary man.

Yet he is not a fool.

Happy and bright,
He thrives in the world.

27 Weary of the vagaries of the mind,
He is at last composed.

He does not know or think,
Or hear or see.

28 Undistracted,
He does not meditate.

Unbound,
He does not seek freedom.

He sees the world,
But knows it is an illusion.

He lives like God.

29 Even when he is still,
The selfish man is busy.

Even when he is busy,
The selfless man is still.

30 He is free.

His mind is unmoved
By trouble or pleasure.

Free from action, desire or doubt,
He is still, and he shines!

31 His mind does not strive
To meditate or to act.

It acts or meditates without purpose.

32 When a fool hears the truth,
He is muddled.

When a wise man hears it,
He goes within.

He may look like a fool,
But he is not muddled.

33 The fool practices concentration
And control of the mind.

But the master is like a man asleep.

He rests in himself
And finds nothing more to do.

34 Striving or still,
The fool never finds peace.

But the master finds it
Just by knowing how things are.

35 In this world
Men try all kinds of paths.

But they overlook the Self,
The Beloved.

Awake and pure,
Flawless and full,
Beyond the world.

36 The fool will never find freedom
By practicing concentration.

But the master never fails.

Just by knowing how things are,
He is free and constant.

37 Because the fool wants to become God,
He never finds him.

The master is already God,
Without ever wishing to be.

38 The fool has no foundation.
Fretting to be free,
He only keeps the world spinning.

But the master cuts at its root,
The root of all suffering.

39 Because the fool looks for peace,
He never finds it.

But the master is always at peace,
Because he understands how things are.

40 If a man looks to the world,
How can he see himself?

The master is never distracted by this or that.

He sees himself,
The Self that never changes.

41 The fool tries to control his mind.
How can he ever succeed?

Mastery always comes naturally
To the man who is wise
And who loves himself.

42 One man believes in existence,
Another says, "There is nothing!"

Rare is the man who believes in neither.

He is free from confusion.

43 The fool may know that the Self
Is pure and indivisible.

But because of his folly,
He never finds it.

He suffers all his life.

44 The mind of a man who longs to be free
Stumbles without support.

But the mind of a man who is already free
Stands on its own.

It is empty of passion.

45 The senses are tigers.

When a timid man catches sight of them,
He runs for safety to the nearest cave,
To practice control and meditation.

46 But a man without desires is a lion.

When the senses see him,
It is they who take flight!

They run away like elephants,
As quietly as they can.

And if they cannot escape,
They serve him like slaves.

47 A man who has no doubts
And whose mind is one with the Self
No longer looks for ways to find freedom.

He lives happily in the world,
Seeing and hearing,
Touching and smelling and tasting.

48 Just by hearing the truth
He becomes spacious
And his awareness pure.

He is indifferent
To striving or stillness.

He is indifferent
To his own indifference.

49 The master is like a child.
He does freely whatever comes his way,
Good or bad.

50 By standing on his own
A man finds happiness.

By standing on his own
A man finds freedom.

By standing on his own
He goes beyond the world.

By standing on his own
He finds the end of the way.

51 When a man realizes
He is neither the doer nor the enjoyer,
The ripples of his mind are stilled.

52 The master's way is unfettered
And free of guile.
He shines.

But for the fool
There is no peace.
His thoughts are full of desire.

53 The master is free of his mind,
And his mind is free.

In this freedom he plays.
He has a wonderful time!

Or he withdraws
And lives in a mountain cave.

54 If the master encounters
A king or a woman
Or someone he dearly loves,
He is without desire.

And when he honors
A god or a holy place
Or a man versed in the scriptures,
There is no longing in his heart.

None at all!

55 He is unperturbed
Even when his servants despise him,
Or his wives, sons, and grandsons mock him.

Even when his whole family makes fun of him,
He is undismayed.

56 For him there is no pain in pain,
No pleasure in pleasure.

Only those who are like him
Can know his exaltation.

57 He has no form.
His form is emptiness.

He is constant and pure.

He has no sense of duty,
Which only binds men to the world.

58 The master fulfills his duties
And is always untroubled.

The fool does nothing
And is always troubled and distracted.

59 The master goes about his business
With perfect equanimity.

He is happy when he sits,
Happy when he talks and eats,
Happy asleep,
Happy coming and going.

60 Because he knows his own nature,
He does what he has to without feeling ruffled
Like ordinary people.

Smooth and shining,
Like the surface of a vast lake.

His sorrows are at an end.

61 The fool is busy
Even when he is still.

Even when he is busy
The master gathers the fruits of stillness.

62 The fool often spurns his possessions.

The master is no longer attached to his body.
So how can he feel attraction or aversion?

63 The awareness of the fool is always limited
By thinking, or by trying not to think.

The awareness of the man who lives within,
Though he may be busy thinking,
Is beyond even awareness itself.

64 The master is like a child.
All his actions are without motive.

He is pure.
Whatever he does, he is detached.

65 He is blessed.
He understands the nature of the Self.
His mind is no longer thirsty.

He is the same under all conditions,
Whatever he sees or hears,
Or smells or touches or tastes.

66 The master is like the sky.
He never changes.

What does the world matter to him,
Or its reflection?

What does he care about seeking,
Or the end of seeking?

67 He is ever the same.
The victory is his.
He has conquered the world.

He is the embodiment
Of his own perfect essence,
By nature one with the infinite.

68 What more is there to say?

He knows the truth.
He has no desire for pleasure or liberation.

At all times, in all places,
He is free from passion.

69 He has given up the duality of the world
Which arises with the mind
And is nothing more than a name.

He is pure awareness.
What is there left for him to do?

70 The man who is pure knows for certain
That nothing really exists;
It is all the work of illusion.

He sees what cannot be seen.
His nature is peace.

71 He does not see the world of appearances.

So what do rules matter to him,
Or dispassion, renunciation, and self-control?

His form is pure and shining light.

72 He does not see the world.

So what does he care for joy or sorrow,
Bondage or liberation?

He is infinite and shining.

73 Before the awakening of understanding
The illusion of the world prevails.
But the master is free of passion.

He has no "I,"
He has no "mine,"
And he shines!

74 He sees that the Self never suffers or dies.

So what does he care for knowledge
Or the world?

Or the feeling "I am the body,"
"The body is mine"?

75 The moment a fool gives up concentration
And his other spiritual practices,
He falls prey to fancies and desires.

76 Even after hearing the truth,
The fool clings to his folly.

He tries hard to look calm and composed,
But inside he is full of cravings.

77 When the truth is understood,
Work falls away.

Though in the eyes of others
The master may seem to work,
In reality he has no occasion
To say or to do anything.

78 He has no fear.
He is always the same.

He has nothing to lose.

For him there is no darkness,
There is no light.

There is nothing at all.

79 He has no being of his own.
His nature cannot be described.

What is patience to him,
Or discrimination or fearlessness?

80 In the eyes of the master
There is nothing at all.

There is no heaven.
There is no hell.

There is no such thing as liberation in life.

What more is there to say?

81 Nothing he hopes to win,
Nothing he fears to lose.

His mind is cool and drenched with nectar.

82 Free from desire,
He neither praises the peaceful
Nor blames the wicked.

The same in joy and sorrow,
He is always happy.

He sees there is nothing to do.

83 He does not hate the world.
He does not seek the Self.

He is free from joy and sorrow.

He is not alive,
And he is not dead.

84 He is not attached to his family.

Free from the desire of the senses,
He does not care about his body.

The master expects nothing,
And he shines.

85 Whatever befalls him,
He is always happy.

He wanders where he will.

And wherever he finds himself
When the sun sets,
There he lies down to rest.

86 He does not care if the body lives or dies.

He is so firmly set in his own being,
He rises above the round of birth and death.

87 He is full of joy.

Attached to nothing,
Free from possessions,
He stands on his own.

His doubts dispelled,
He wanders where he will,
Never setting one thing against another.

88 The master shines.

He never says "mine."
Gold, stone, earth—
They are all the same to him.

He is not bound by sloth,
Nor consumed by his own activity.

He has severed the knots which bind his heart.

89 Who can compare with him?

Indifferent to everything,
He is happy and he is free.

There is not the least desire in his heart.

90 Only the man without desire
Sees without seeing,
Speaks without speaking,
Knows without knowing.

91 In his view of things
Good and evil have melted away.

A king or a beggar,
Whoever is free from desire shines!

92 He is utterly without guile.
He has found his way.
He is simplicity itself.

He cares nothing for restraint,
Or abandon.

He has no interest in finding the truth.

93 He has no desires.
He rests happily in the Self.

His sorrows are over.
How can anyone tell what he feels inside?

94 Even when he is sound asleep,
He is not asleep.

Even when he is dreaming,
He does not dream.

Even when he is awake,
He is not awake.

Step by step,
Whatever befalls him,
He is happy.

95 He thinks without thinking.
He feels without feeling.

He is intelligent,
But he has no mind.

He has personality,
But with no thought for himself.

96 He is not happy,
Nor is he sad.

He is not detached,
Nor is he bound.

He is not free,
Nor does he seek freedom.

He is not this.
He is not that.

97 Amid distractions,
He is undistracted.

In meditation,
He does not meditate.

Foolish,
He is not a fool.

Knowing everything,
He knows nothing.

98 He always lives within.
He is everywhere the same.

Action or duty are nothing to him.

Because he is free from desire,
He never worries about what he has done
Or has not done.

99 Blame does not not disturb him,
Nor does praise delight him.

He neither rejoices in life,
Nor fears death.

100 His mind is calm.

Never seeking the solitude of the forest,
Nor running from the crowd.

Always and everywhere,
He is one and the same.

19 *My Own Splendor*

1 With the pincers of truth I have plucked
From the dark corners of my heart
The thorn of many judgments.

2 I sit in my own splendor.

Wealth or pleasure,
Duty or discrimination,
Duality or nonduality,
What are they to me?

3 What is yesterday,
Tomorrow,
Or today?

What is space,
Or eternity?

I sit in my own radiance.

4 What is the Self,
Or the not-Self?

What is thinking,
Or not thinking?

What is good or evil?

I sit in my own splendor.

5 I sit in my own radiance,
And I have no fear.

Waking,
Dreaming,
Sleeping,
What are they to me?

Or even ecstasy?

6 What is far or near,
Outside or inside,
Gross or subtle?

I sit in my own splendor.

7 Dissolving the mind,
Or the highest meditation,
The world and all its works,
Life or death,
What are they to me?

I sit in my own radiance.

8 Why talk of wisdom,
The three ends of life,
Or oneness?

Why talk of these!

Now I live in my heart.

20 *I Am Shiva*

1 I am fulfilled.

The elements of nature,
The body and the senses,
What are they to me?

Or the mind?

What is emptiness or despair?

2 What are holy books,
Or knowledge of the Self,
Or the mind,
Even when it is free of the senses?

Or happiness,
Or freedom from desire?

I am always
One without two.

3 Knowledge or ignorance,
Freedom or bondage,
What are they?

What is "I,"
Or "mine,"
Or "this"?

Or the form of the true Self?

4 I am always one.

What do I care for freedom
In life or in death,
Or for my present karma?

5 I am always
Without I.

So where is the one
Who acts or enjoys?

And what is the rising
Or the vanishing of thought?

What is the invisible world,
Or the visible?

6 In my heart I am one.

What is this world?

Who seeks freedom,
Or wisdom or oneness?

Who is bound or free?

7 In my heart I am one.

What is creation,
Or dissolution?

What is seeking,
And the end of seeking?

Who is the seeker?
What has he found?

8 I am forever pure.

What do I care who knows,
What is known,
Or how it is known?

What do I care for knowledge?

What do I care what is,
Or what is not?

9 I am forever still.

What are joy or sorrow,
Distraction or concentration,
Understanding or delusion?

10 I am always without thought.

What is happiness or grief?

What is here and now,
Or beyond?

11 I am forever pure.

What is illusion,
Or the world?

What is the little soul,
Or God Himself?

12 One without two,
I am always the same.

I sit in my heart.

13 What need is there
For striving or stillness?

What is freedom or bondage?

What are holy books or teachings?

What is the purpose of life?

Who is the disciple,
And who is the master?

14 For I have no bounds.

I am Shiva.

Nothing arises in me,
In whom nothing is single,
Nothing is double.

Nothing is,
Nothing is not.

What more is there to say?

Notes

Throughout my translation of the *Ashtavakra Gita* and in the following notes, I have rendered familiar personal names (e.g., Vishnu, Shankara, Ashtavakra) as well as the names of a few major scriptures (the *Bhagavad Gita,* the Upanishads) in the popular simplified form, which can easily be pronounced by anyone. In citing the Sanskrit text in Richard Hauschild's edition (Berlin: Akademie Verlag, 1967), I use the standard scholarly transliteration (as does Dr. Brockington in his foreword).

The notes following are keyed to verse numbers.

Chapter 1. The Self

1 Except here and in a few other verses (1.2, 14; 9.2; 12.4; 15.8, 12; 16.1, 2) there is no clear or natural colloquy and no attempt to distinguish the voices of King Janaka and Ashtavakra. On the contrary, a single voice, speaking with undisputed authority, dominates every chapter. For these reasons I have dispensed with the fiction of a dramatic dialogue, except for the opening question.

2 This is one of the few verses in which the poet recommends following, rather than transcending, conventional virtue. For this reason some commentators suggest that it is spurious. Yet from time to time the poet strikes a compromise with the conditional world of formal *sadhana* to propose, for instance, the benefits of constancy in meditation (cf. 1.13; 10.1, 3, 5, 7; 17.1; 18.33). Indeed there is a certain playful irony in the way in which he expresses the paradoxes which arise from viewing the relative world of spiritual striving from the vantage point of a strict monism.

3 The poet refers to the five elements which according to Sāṃkhya doctrine constitute the phenomenal world.

4 *At once.* Skt. *adhunā,* "at once, now." This sense of immediacy is characteristic of the poet. We find it again at the end of chapter 10 when he urges the seeker to give up his striving. "It is time to stop. Now." Sometimes his "nows" are perhaps no more than "*pāda*-stuffers," that is, they may simply serve to fill out the line. But often they express a true sense of urgency, a discriminating impatience, in which all experience is gathered urgently into the present moment. The Self may be realized all at once.

5 *Stages of life.* Skt. *āśrama,* the four traditional stages of life: *brahmacarya,* youth and study; *gārhasthya,* keeping house; *vānaprastha,* retreat in the forest; *saṃnyāsa,* renunciation.

Free. Skt. *asaṅga,* "free (from material, emotional or spiritual attachments)."

The witness of all things. Skt. *sākṣī.* The idea of the Self as the single witness is common in the Upanishads, but rare in the *Bhagavad Gita.* (Cf. *draṣṭā,* 1.3, 5, 7, 12.)

10 In the literature of Advaita Vedānta, this image of the snake and the rope is a stock one, together with the images of mother-of-pearl/silver and water/mirage, for the illusory nature of the world, which exists only as a false appearance when through ignorance we fail to identify ourselves with the one Self, indivisible and formless. For an authoritative discussion of this and other stock imagery, see Karl H. Potter, *Advaita Vedānta up to Śaṃkara and His Pupils* (Princeton, N.J.: Princeton Univ. Press, 1981).

11 There is a strong echo here of the opening verses of the *Dhammapada.* Other possible references to Buddhist scripture and thought are at 2.23–25; 18.42, 63; 20.1.

13 *Exalted awareness.* Skt. *kūṭasthaṃ,* "standing on a mountain top," suggesting the aloofness and remoteness of the Self (cf. 20.12). For further discussion, see J. L. Brockington, "Mysticism in the Epics," in *Perspectives in Indian Religion: Papers in Honour of Karl Werner,* edited by Peter Connolly (Delhi: Sri Satguru Publications, 1986), pp. 9–20.

17 *Limitless.* Skt. *nirbhara,* "without weight, measure," hence "limitless, unburdened."

Serene. Skt. *śītalā.*

Unperturbed. Skt. *akṣubdha.*

19 The image here has given rise to some confusion. Does the poet intend the idea of superimposition *(adhyāsa, āropa)* as in the stock figures of the snake/rope, silver/mother-of-pearl, mirage/water; or all-pervasiveness of the Self *(sarvagatam)* in harmony with the image in the concluding verse? I prefer the second interpretation.

Chapter 2. Awareness

1, 3 See note to 1.1

3 *I have a special gift.* Skt. *kutaścit kauśalād eva,* "somehow indeed by (some) skill."

4, 5, 6, 9 See discussion by Karl H. Potter mentioned in note to 1.10.

11–14 In this unabashed Self-adoration, spiritual rapture and austere discrimination speak with one voice. It is hard to convey in English the force of this conjunction which, next to the dualist litanies of praise of conventional Christianity and Hinduism, may sound strangely inflated. However, in the ecstatic self-adoration of the mystics one finds not uncommonly other voices speaking from the same absolute identification with the Self, with as absolute a sense of wonder and humility.

I live beyond all distinctions. Skt. *nirvikalpa,* "without distinctions, changes; choiceless, undifferentiated." This term distinguishes pure, choiceless awareness from *savikalpa samādhi,* in which awareness is still compromised. The poet uses it often, as does Gaudapada before him. It is not found in the Upanishads or in the *Bhagavad Gita.*

17 *Bound.* Skt. *upādhi,* from the verbal root "to place over," denotes in the language of Advaita a limiting adjunct, a superimposition limiting the oneness of the Self. It also means "disguise, mirage."

21 To the master who sees everything as one, the teeming mass of humanity seems like a wilderness in which everything appears as it is, alone, all one, empty of form.

22 *Thirst for life.* Skt. *jīvite spṛhā,* that is, for life as an individual being, *jīva,* in whom the desire for individuation arises from ignorance of its essential identity with the indivisible Self.

23–25 The poet, and Shankara before him, may have drawn this image (ocean/being, waves/world) from Ashvaghosha, an early master of Mahāyāna Buddhism. (Cf. 6.2; 7.1, 2, 3; 15.11, 18.)

Chapter 3. Wisdom

2 *Where the senses whirl.* Skt. *viṣayabhramagocare,* "in the field of the whirl of the senses."

3 *Yourself as That.* Skt. *so 'ham asmīti,* "I am That." Cf. the familiar declaration of the Upanishads *(sa ahaṃ, ahaṃ asmi).*

5 *The man . . . in himself.* These words echo the *Bhagavad Gita* (6.29), are repeated at 15.6, and appear again in slightly different form at 6.4, to express both the immanence and the transcendence of the Self.

9 *The absolute Self.* Skt. *kevalaṃ,* "absolute." The sense here is of absolute aloneness, the splendid isolation of the Self, as used also by Patanjali and in the later Upanishads.

11, 13 *With clear and steady insight.* Skt. *dhīradhīh.* The poet is playing with two different terms, "insight" and "resolve," to characterize the master, *dhīra* (cf. 18.7 and note), as one possessing a clear, calm, and steady insight.

12 *In despair.* Skt. *nairāśya,* "hopelessness, despair, non-expectation." Two readings seem possible; the first is literal, the second, adopted by Swami Nityaswarupanananda in his version, prefers "the state of freedom in which nothing is expected," hence "liberation." I have chosen the first.

He, him. Skt. *mahātmanaḥ,* "great self, soul." Sometimes I omit the poet's reference to "the master," preferring for the sake of fluency the third-person pronoun. I choose also to translate as "the master" a number of words (see note to 18.7) with which the poet varies and makes more colorful his text. I do so for the sake of fluency and simplicity; it is very difficult to convey the exact flavor of each title without sounding wordy and awkward.

Chapter 4. The True Seeker

4, 6 *ydṛcchaya varttamānaṃ,* "doing as he wishes," and *yad vetti tat sa kurute,* "he acts accordingly," together express the independence and spontaneity of the master, qualities further developed in the poet's portrait of the *jīvanmukta,* the man liberated while still living, in Chapter 18.

5 *The four kinds of being.* They are gods, men, animals, and plants; or, those born from a womb, from eggs, from sweat, and from sprouting. In other words, the whole of creation.

6 *The Lord of all creation.* Skt. *jagadīśvaraṃ,* "the lord of the world." As at 11.2, 14.3, and 15.8, the poet identifies the Self with *īśvara* ("ruler, king; husband; supreme personal God; Siva"), following perhaps the example of the *Bhagavad Gita* and several Upanishads. Elsewhere he identifies *ātman, paramātman* with *bhagavān* ("lord"). This is hardly a compromise with theism, as some commentators suggest, but rather reinforces the strictness of his monism, by submitting all, even God, to a true and irreducible identity with the one Self.

Chapter 5. Dissolving

1 *Dissolve.* Skt. *layaṃ,* "melting, dissolving." In *laya yoga* the seeker attempts through techniques of breathing or meditation the dissolution of his identification with the senses, the mind and the phenomenal world, and of all the attachments which arise from his original mistake of individuation. Patanjali's system stresses *prāṇāyāma,* breathing. The *Yogatattva Upanishad* suggests that the mind may be melted only by constancy in meditation. Ashtavakra's view in this chapter is that dissolving comes about only by direct acknowledgment of the purity and perfection of the Self. But in the next chapter he insists that a true understanding makes even the need for dissolving absurd. For after all, what is there to melt?

Body and mind. Skt. *saṃghāta,* "pushing together, cluster, aggregate." The poet refers here to the illusory cluster of the body and mind which constitutes the little self.

Chapter 6. Knowledge

1 See also 1.10, 19. The figures here are so familiar that the poet does not even trouble to explain them. They are found in the Upanishads, in Shankara, and in Gaudapada's *Māṇḍūkya Kārikā.* Some commentators suppose that Gaudapada borrowed from the Ashtavakra poet. It is much likelier that Ashtavakra echoes Gaudapada, whose *asparśa yoga* he reforms and refines.

Nothing to accept . . . to reject. The idea of attraction (*graha*) and aversion (*tyāga*), which here provides the poet with his refrain, also echoes Gaudapada.

Chapter 9. Dispassion

1 *Dispassion.* Skt. *nirveda.* The more literal meaning is "disgust," and the word is usually stronger than the more familiar *vairāgya* (10.3), "without passion, desire," and hence "detachment". Cf. *anādara* (10.1), "lack of attention to/concern for, disregard"; *asaṃsakti* (10.4), "absence of attachment toward, absence of strong attachments." In the *Bhagavad Gita, nirveda* means "detachment from the fruits of action" and, generally, "nonattachment." The Ashtavakra poet here and elsewhere (*mūdha,* "fool" at 18.39 and *passim*) prefers strong language.

3 *Beneath contempt.* Skt. *ninditaṃ,* "blameworthy, despised, inauspicious," hence "worthy of contempt, contemptible."

Threefold affliction. Skt. *tāpatritayadūṣitam.* Misery is threefold because it originates internally, from the individual himself; externally, from other beings; or supernaturally, from the gods or fate. This convention expresses, of course, the idea of all forms of sorrow.

6 *With dispassion.* Skt. *nirvedasamatāyuktyā,* "dispassion, equanimity, reason." My version is a little informal.

7 *In the shifting . . . pure form.* Skt. *paśya bhūtavikārāṃs tvaṃ,* "see in the modification of the gross elements the primary elements themselves." The idea is that everything in nature evolves from a simpler form, an archetype. In meditation the seeker reverses this evolutionary process, returning to a state of primal simplicity, and at last melting back into the one Self.

tatkṣaṇā, "at once." I have translated this by rendering the verbs as imperatives. (Cf. 1.4, 10.8, etc.) Again the poet wishes to stress the urgency of the task, and at the same time he suggests that illumination is to be had all at once. I have translated *adya,* "now," in the next verse in the same way.

8 *False impressions.* Skt. *vāsanā.* Often translated "desires," it rather means "sense impressions," "mental images," "motivations," even "habit patterns." The world is just a bad habit—so give it up, now!

Chapter 10. Desire

1, 7 *Kāma, artha, dharma,* "pleasure, prosperity, duty." These are the traditional *trivarga,* the three basic drives of human life. A fourth is often added, *mokṣa,* "freedom," to which the Ashtavakra poet adds a variant, *vivekitā,* "discrimination" (18.12; 19.2). He makes it plain that all four, even the desire for liberation, have to be surrendered, since each is an attachment to the illusion of separation.

5 *Cold and lifeless.* Skt. *jaḍaṃ,* "cold, cool, rigid, numb; dimmed, dull; stupid, imbecile; inanimate, lifeless, inert." I have chosen in my translation to spell out some of these senses.

Chapter 11. Stillness

1 *When you know this.* Skt. *niścayī,* "knowing for certain," rather than simply "knowing." The poet uses this emphatic refrain to stitch his chapter together.

5 *Fear.* Skt. *cintā,* "thought, reflection" or "anxiety, fear." Both readings are possible.

Chapter 12. Fulfillment

1 *I am here.* Skt. *āham āsthitah,* "I rest, stand (in myself)." Cf. *svastha* (17.14; 18.50, 63, 98), "resting, standing in one's own (self)," "established in the true Self"; also "self-reliant, independent." *Svāsthya* (13.1; 16.1, 11), "abidance in the Self." *Svātantrya* (18.50), "independence, standing on his own." In the *Bhagavad Gita, svastha* occurs once (14.24), signifying indifference to pleasure and pain, and detachment from the world by turning inward. Gaudapada also appears to use the term only once (*Māṇḍūkya Kārikā* 13.47). The Ashtavakra poet favors and promotes the term, which is his crucial idiom for the state of awareness of the unconditioned Self. It is, however, difficult to translate without sounding stilted, and I have taken some liberties with it.

1, 3, 5, 7 Here the poet makes most strongly his point that even meditation, as based upon the illusion of separation, must be surrendered. Elsewhere (6.2; 17.18; 18.16, 17, 33) he explains that it is not so much meditation itself as attachment to its practice which obstructs the seeker.

5 *The four stages of life.* See note to 1.5.

8 Notice how, as with *niścayī* in the last chapter, the poet binds together his verses with an emphatic refrain, and with a series of forceful epigrams, until the last verse, with its own peculiarly compelling epigram, and its own rhyming refrain.

Chapter 13. Happiness

1 In this chapter the poet again advises the seeker to detach himself from the forms and conventions of his search. The true seeker renounces nothing, since there is truly nothing to renounce. Secure in this knowledge, he is happy, and his happiness, as the refrain insists, is one of the few conditions the poet allows of his unqualified oneness.

Chapter 14. The Fool

1 *Without thinking.* Skt. *pramāda,* "negligence, carelessness, inattention, heedlessness, intoxication." The poet is perhaps playing

with several overlapping meanings of the words, to express the master's carefree, reckless, thoughtless attitude to the fluctuations and inconstancy of the mind, from the bondage of which he has freed himself. My translation, "without thinking," while possibly too informal, is designed to convey the playful conjunction of "thoughtless," "careless," and "empty of thought."

2 *The thieving senses.* Skt. *viṣayadasyavaḥ,* "objects of the thieving senses."

3 *God . . . all things.* Skt. *sākṣipuruṣe paramātmani ceśvare,* "God, the witness of all things, supreme spirit, the infinite Self, the Lord." This is the only use of *puruṣa,* "higher personal principle, universal soul, supreme spirit," in the *Ashtavakra Gita,* though the term is familiar in the *Bhagavad Gita* and the Upanishads. The poet takes delight here in summing up all the main terms for God and reducing them to a common and indivisible identity with the Self.

4 *Within, free of thought.* Skt. *antarvikalpaśūnyasya,* "empty of thoughts within." *Vikalpa,* here "discursive thoughts." The poet contrasts the outer appearance and inner nature of the master. Because he is literally empty-headed he may seem foolish. But this vacancy is, of course, the emptiness of Self-realization. The poet may also be suggesting "empty of contrivance, free from doubt." The master is truly ingenuous, and his faith is unshakeable.

Chapter 15. The Clear Space of Awareness

4 *Pure awareness.* Skt. *cidrūpo,* "the form of awareness." Cf. *cidrūpa* (1.3), *cinmātra* (1.13), *cinmaya* (15.59), *sphūrtimātra* (11.8, 15.7), *bodhātma* (15.5), *tattvabodha* (15.3), *cidākāśa* (15.15), *jñānasvarūpa* (15.8), etc. The poet wrings many compounds out of these basic terms for "pure awareness," all as synonyms for "the Self," *ātman.* Some he makes peculiarly his own, others are suggested by the Upanishads, Gaudapada and Shankara, for instance, *citsvarūpa, ātmajyotiḥ, vijñānaṃ.*

4, 5, 6, 9, 15, 18, 19 Here, as in Chapter 13, the poet makes a refrain of his command to the seeker to be, above all, happy. It is perhaps his single most pressing instruction. Without constantly looking to his own happiness, a man will never find himself. Nothing is discovered in sorrow. As he has said at 9.3, suffering is merely contemptible. At the end of the chapter he sums it all up in one of his most striking commands: "Live in the happiness/Of your own nature,/Which is happiness itself."

8, 12 *Child.* Skt. *tāta.* See notes to 1.1, 2. These are among the few verses which support the dialogue form.

12 *How could you.* Skt. *kasya kathaṃ kutra,* "whose, how, where." I have chosen to translate these interrogatives with the rhetorical "How could you!"

15 *ayaṃ so 'ham ayaṃ nāham.* The reference here is to the conventional mantra "I am He," "I am not this, I am not that." The practice of mantra is dualistic, and must be surrendered.

Rid yourself . . . purpose. Skt. *niḥsaṅkalpaḥ,* "without volitional activity, intention (toward any external), free from intentions (toward the objects of the world)." That is, free of intentions of the kind the mind needs in order to construct or invent the phenomenal world. The master is without any such purpose, and so he remains established in the single Self, free of all illusion.

20 *Once and for all.* Skt. *sarvatra,* "everywhere, in all cases, always." Again, the poet dismisses meditation as bound to thought, even though its intention is to dissolve the mind. Since there is no mind, any intention to dissolve it is essentially futile, and only serves the illusion of the separate self. See notes to 12.1, 3, 5, 7.

Chapter 16. Forget Everything

9 *Renounce desire.* Skt. *vītarāgo,* "free from passion, worldly desire." I have introduced an imperative here to make clear the practicality of the distinction which the poet suggests between attachment to the world, and attachment to attachment itself.

Chapter 17. Beyond All

1 *His practice.* Skt. *yogābhyāsa,* "the practice of yoga." The seeker may abandon meditation only after he has gathered the fruit of long practice. See notes to 12.1, 3, 5, 7.

3 *The senses.* Skt. *visayāḥ.* Here I have translated "senses." Literally, "objects of the senses," hence "the things of the world" (17.17).

6 *Duty or liberation.* Skt. *dharmārthakāmamokṣeṣu,* "duty, prosperity, pleasure, liberation." The four basic drives of human life. See notes to 10.1, 7.

9, 10 *His eyes are empty.* Skt. *śūnyā dṛṣṭir,* "his gaze is empty." Here the poet begins to warm to his description, extended throughout the next chapter, of the *jīvanmukta,* the master who is liberated while still living.

12 By repeating a *pāda* from verse 8, the poet stitches together his chapter with devices at once mnemonic, formulaic, and lyrical.

14 *He stays in his heart.* Skt. *svastho.* Here, and *passim,* my translation is somewhat informal. See note to 12.1.

16 *Compassion, humility.* Skt. *kāruṇyaṃ, dīnata.* The master has transcended even such laudable qualities as compassion and humility, since even they are qualifications of his oneness.

Chapter 18. The Master

7 *The master.* Skt. *dhīro,* "wise man, master." Of the many titles the poet uses for "master," this is the most common. He uses it nearly twenty times in this chapter alone. (Cf. *dhī,* "thought, understanding, insight, devotion"; *dhīra,* "lasting, steady, resolute"; *dhīra,* "thoughtful, wise, skilled"). His other most frequent title/epithet is *yogin,* "devotee of yoga," which occurs here seven times. He also favors *budha,* "wise man, awakened being, sage" (from *budh,* "to awaken, bloom, reveal, arouse, cause to open, be aware, come to understand, elicit a perfume," etc.). He twice uses *mahāśaya,* "noble, high-minded"; twice *śāntadhī,* "of composed understanding"; twice *mahātman,* "great soul"; and once each *udāra,* "noble exalted"; *muni,* "inspired or ecstatic man, one who has taken the vow of silence, seer, ascetic,

sage"; *kuśala,* "fitting, skillful, expert, experienced"; *jīvanmukta,* "free while living"; *mukta,* "free"; *prājña,* "wise, sensible"; *ṛju,* "straight, right, just, honest"; *sūri,* "wise man, great scholar"; *jña,* "knowing, understanding." I have spelled these out in order to give some idea of the shades of meaning in each epithet/title. Like most translators, I have rendered nearly all the words with a single term, preferring "master" to "wise man," etc. These terms are mostly adjectival and do not necessarily carry any more weight than the longer compounds with which the poet also attempts to describe the ineffable nature of the master. See the following note on negative epithets.

8 *Free of desire.* Skt. *niṣkāma,* "without desire, lust." Attempting to name the unnameable character of the master, the poet resorts most commonly to a device of negative litanies, by which he establishes what the master is not. I have gathered some of these together in order to better acquaint the reader with their various shades of meaning, to which I could hardly do justice in my translation: *nirañjana,* "without stain"; *nirviśeṣa,* "without differences"; *nirupādhi,* "without limitations"; *niṣkriya,* "without action"; *niḥsvabhāva,* "without natural attributes, human limits"; *niṣprapañca,* "without relativity, without relation to the natural world"; *nīrasa,* "without flavor, desire"; *nirvikalpa,* "without choice, fluctuation"; *nirvikāra,* "without spot, stain, change"; *nirvasana,* "without desires, fancies"; *nirnimitta,* "without motive, intention"; *nirākula,* "without distraction"; *nirālamba,* "without support, any supporting object"; *niḥśaṅka,* "without doubts"; *nirakara,* "without body, form"; *nirāmaya,* "without disease, flaw"; *nistarṣamanasa,* "without mind"; *nirmama,* "without mine"; *nirahaṃkāra,* "without I"; *nirātaṅka, "without fear"; nirvyāja,* "without deceit." There are many more of these negatives.

The poet is sparer in his use of positive epithets. At 18.35 we learn that the master is *śuddhaṃ buddhaṃ priyaṃ pūṛṇaṃ,* "pure, awakened, beloved, fulfilled." Running together the poet's terms for "master," we learn that he is wise, resolute, at one with the Self, awakened, noble, peaceful, exalted, inspired, skillful, free, of deep understanding, upright, and so on. No doubt to the poet's contemporary audience all these terms would have flavors which are now partly lost to us.

8 *God.* Skt. *brahmeti.* (Cf. 18.16, 28, 37; 20.11; *passim.*) See notes to 4.6 and 14.3. My translation "God" may obscure for the Western reader the impersonality of the concept. For an excellent discussion of *brahman* and *īśvara* see the commentary by Swami Prabhavananda and Christopher Isherwood on Shankara's *Crest-Jewel of Discrimination* (Hollywood: Vedanta Press, 1947).

12 *Discrimination.* Skt. *vivekitā.* The poet substitutes "discrimination" for *mokṣa,* "liberation, release," the more usual term. See notes to 10.1, 7; 17.6. True discrimination leads spontaneously to liberation.

32 I have added "But he is not muddled" to complete the sense.

34 *Just by knowing . . . are.* Skt. *tattvaniścayanamātreṇa,* "just by knowing Thatness for certain." Cf. *vijñānamātreṇa* (18.36), "just by knowing"; *tattvaṃ viniścitya* (18.39), "knowing for certain Thatness"; *vastuśravaṇamātreṇa* (18.48), "just by hearing the truth." In these crucial verses the poet stresses that the Self is realized only by *vijñāna, anubhava,* by direct unmediated perception of Reality, that is, by an intuitive illumination for which no amount of striving can prepare the seeker.

37 The desire for God is perhaps the final attachment. But it too must be exposed as just another obstruction, a folly arising from the illusion of separation.

42 Here, as elsewhere, the poet seems to reject the propositions of the Buddhist Mādhyamika school. The true master acknowledges neither the existence nor the nothingness of the self.

69 According to Sāṃkhya ideas concerning the natural evolution of the phenomenal world, *mahat,* literally "the great one, the great principle," is an alternative term for *buddhi,* "consciousness," the first evolute from *prakṛti,* "nature." An adequate translation seems impossible. But the meaning is simple enough: the master has dissolved the duality of the world in all aspects of its evolution.

Chapter 19. My Own Splendor

5 *Ecstasy.* Skt. *turīyaṃ,* "the fourth state." Conventional Vedantic psychology, as expressed in the Upanishads, recognized four

states of consciousness: waking, dreaming, dreamless sleep and "the fourth state" of ecstatic transcendence. But this too depends on duality, and is just another illusion.

8 *In my heart.* Skt. *mamātmani,* "in my own Self." My translation is again somewhat informal.

Chapter 20. I Am Shiva

1 *The elements . . . the senses.* Skt. *kva bhutāni, kvendriyāṇi.* In Sāṃkhya terminology the *bhutas* are the elements, the *indriyas* are the senses. See G. J. Larson, *Classical Sāṃkhya,* 2d ed. (New Delhi: Motilal Banarsidass, 1979).

3 *The form of the true Self.* Skt. *svarūpasya kva rūpitā,* "where is there any attribute to the nature of the Self?" I have translated rather freely as "What is the form of the true Self?"

4 *My present karma.* Skt. *prārabdhāni karmāṇi.* That is, the karma of his present life, which the *jīvanmukti* works out spontaneously and without intention or effort.

5 Skt. *kvāparokṣaṃ phalaṃ va kva. Aparokṣa,* "not invisible, perceptible," does not supply the semantic contrast with *phala,* "fruit (of action)," suggested by the double *kva.* Another possible reading might be *kva parokṣaṃ phalaṃ vā kva,* in which *parokṣa,* "invisible, beyond the eye," provides a suitable contrast. Indeed, this reading, and the first alternative proposed at 20.9, are supported by MS e 107 (6) and MS c 223 (4) (Chandra Shum Shere Collection, Bodleian Library, Oxford), respectively.

9 *Delusion.* Skt. *nirbodhaḥ.* "Folly" fails to supply the suggested contrast. Better readings are *nibodhaḥ,* "understanding," or *nibudhaḥ,* "awakening."

11 *God Himself.* Skt. *tadbrahma.* Even God is just another mental fiction.

14 Skt. *śivasya me.* While this may be purely adjectival, "of me who am blessed," I have chosen to translate it as "I am Shiva" because the poet was almost certainly Shaivite, and it is not unlikely that at this climactic moment he chose to salute Shiva. He can hardly have worried that his monistic argument, which he has so unswervingly promoted, could at this late point be in any way compromised.

Also in SHAMBHALA DRAGON EDITIONS

The Art of War, by Sun Tzu. Translated by Thomas Cleary.

Bodhisattva of Compassion: The Mystical Tradition of Kuan Yin, by John Blofeld.

Buddha in the Palm of Your Hand, by Ösel Tendzin. Foreword by Chögyam Trungpa.

The Buddhist I Ching, by Chih-hsu Ou-i. Translated by Thomas Cleary.

Cutting Through Spiritual Materialism, by Chögyam Trungpa.

Dakini Teachings: Padmasambhava's Oral Instructions to Lady Tsogyal, by Padmasambhava. Translated by Erik Pema Kunsang.

The Dawn of Tantra, by Herbert V. Guenther & Chögyam Trungpa.

The Experience of Insight: A Simple and Direct Guide to Buddhist Meditation, by Joseph Goldstein.

Glimpses of Abhidharma, by Chögyam Trungpa.

The Hundred Thousand Songs of Milarepa (two volumes). Translated by Garma C. C. Chang.

I Ching: The Tao of Organization, by Cheng Yi. Translated by Thomas Cleary.

I Ching Mandalas: A Program of Study for The Book of Changes. Translated & edited by Thomas Cleary.

Mastering the Art of War, by Zhuge Liang & Liu Ji. Translated & edited by Thomas Cleary.

The Myth of Freedom, by Chögyam Trungpa.

Nine-Headed Dragon River, by Peter Matthiessen.

Returning to Silence: Zen Practice in Daily Life, by Dainin Katagiri. Foreword by Robert Thurman.

Seeking the Heart of Wisdom: The Path of Insight Meditation, by Joseph Goldstein & Jack Kornfield. Foreword by H. H. the Dalai Lama.

Shambhala: The Sacred Path of the Warrior, by Chögyam Trungpa.

The Spiritual Teaching of Ramana Maharshi, by Ramana Maharshi. Foreword by C. G. Jung.

The Tantric Mysticism of Tibet, by John Blofeld.

Tao Teh Ching, by Lao Tzu. Translated by John C. H. Wu.

The Tibetan Book of the Dead: The Great Liberation through Hearing in the Bardo. Translated with commentary by Francesca Fremantle & Chögyam Trungpa.

The Vimalakirti Nirdesa Sutra. Translated & edited by Charles Luk. Foreword by Taizan Maezumi Roshi.

Berkeley CA

[SKI Matu]

9 781570 626432